NATIONAL GEOGRAPHIC

Wind Power

Pat Malone

What makes waves crash
onto the shore?

Wind Power!

When the wind blows
hard, it makes big waves.

What makes trees grow bent over?

WIND POWER!

When trees grow in places
where there is always
a strong wind,
the trees grow sideways.

What scatters seeds
far and wide?

WIND POWER!

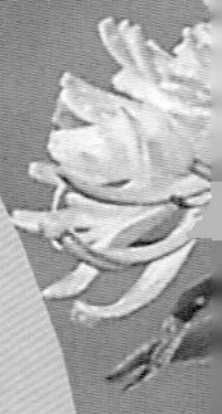

Wind blows the seeds
of many plants.
This helps plants to grow
in new places.

What moves sand dunes?

15

WIND POWER!

Sand dunes are
always moving.
Wind blows sand
to new places.

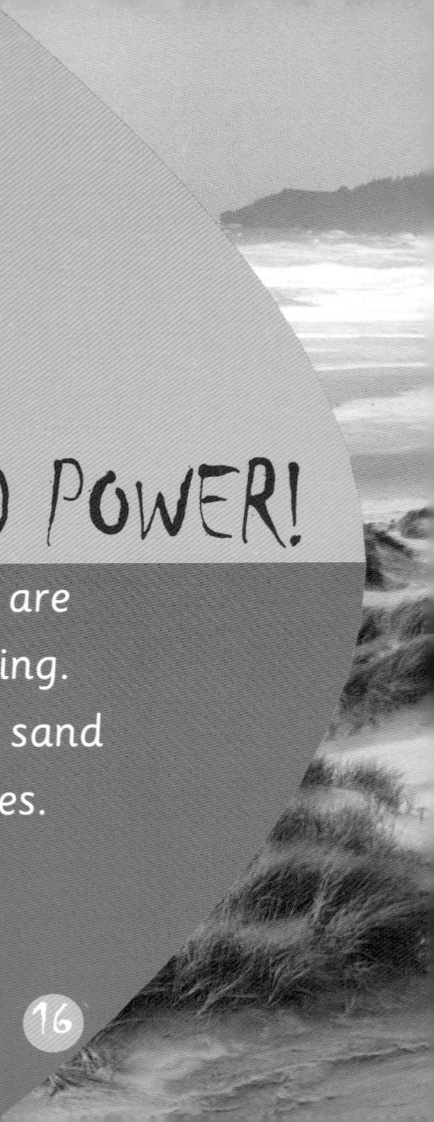

What turns these big blades?

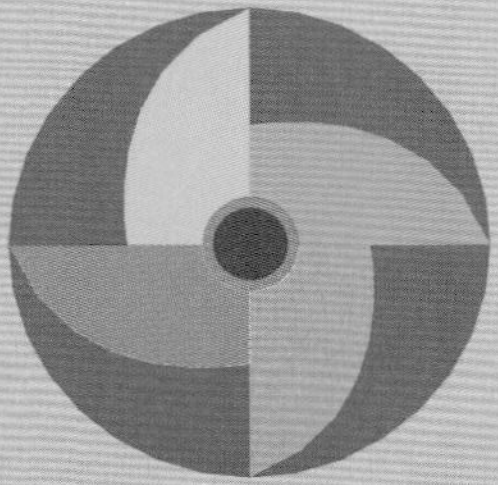

WIND POWER!

Wind turns the blades
of a windmill.
The spinning blades
make power for us to use.

What fills the sails
and blows this boat along

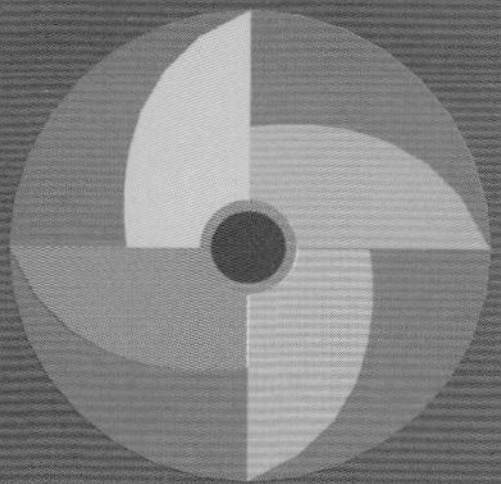